Egyptian Mummies

Coloring Pages for Kids and Kids at Heart

Hands-On Art History

Published in the United States by Hands-On Art History. For bulk sales, email blueivypress@gmail.com.

Egyptian Mummies
Coloring Pages for Kids and Kids at Heart
Hands-On Art History —1st ed.
ISBN 978-1-948344-61-6

FREE COLORING PAGES

Sign up to get free art-related coloring pages
delivered to your inbox each month!

www.HandsOnArtHistory.com

Join the Coloring Club!

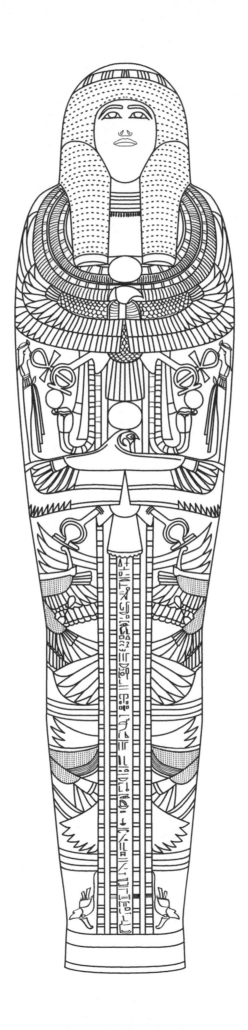

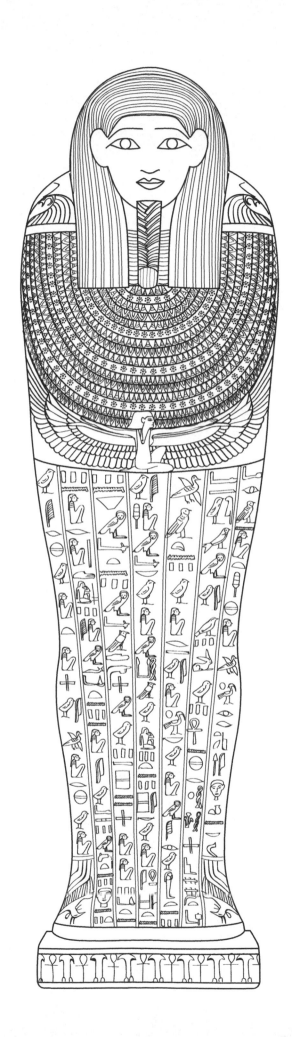

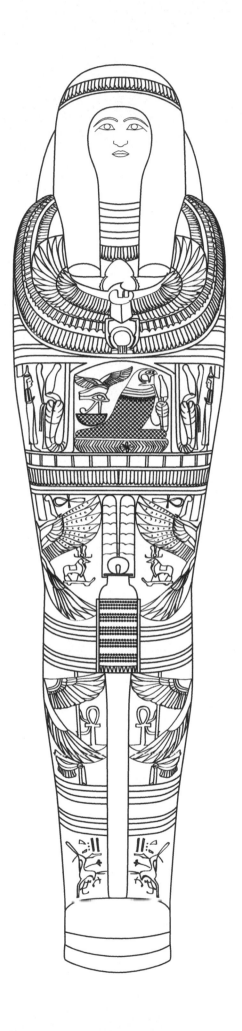

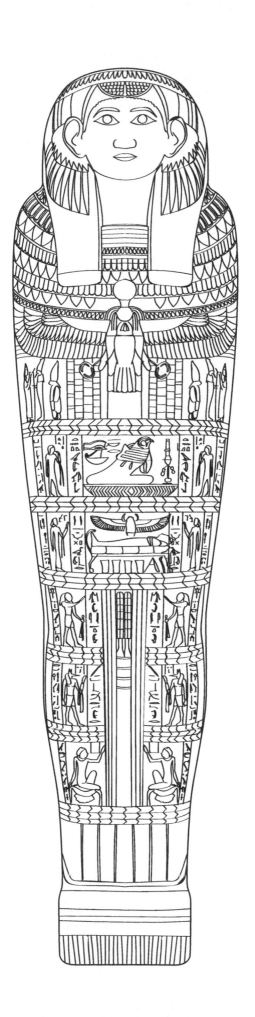

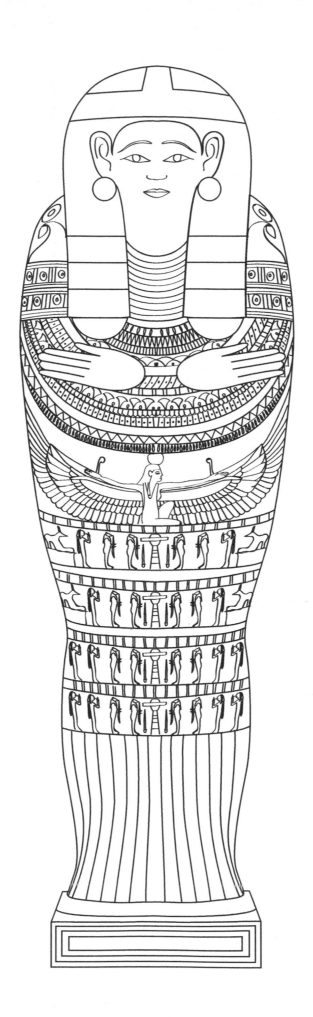

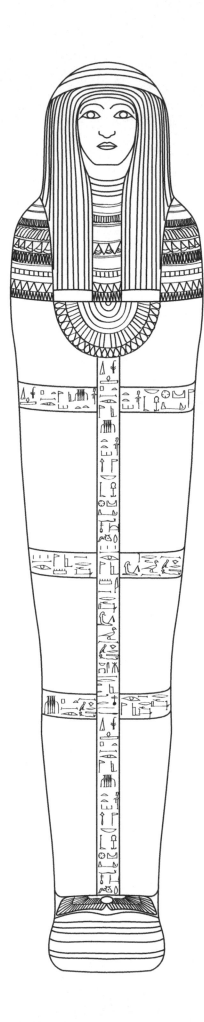

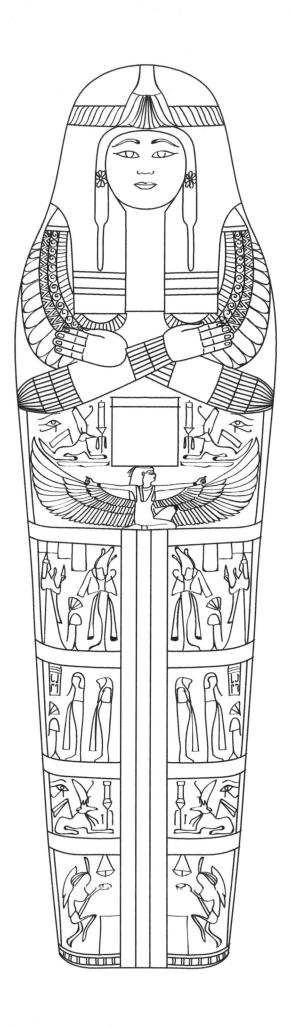

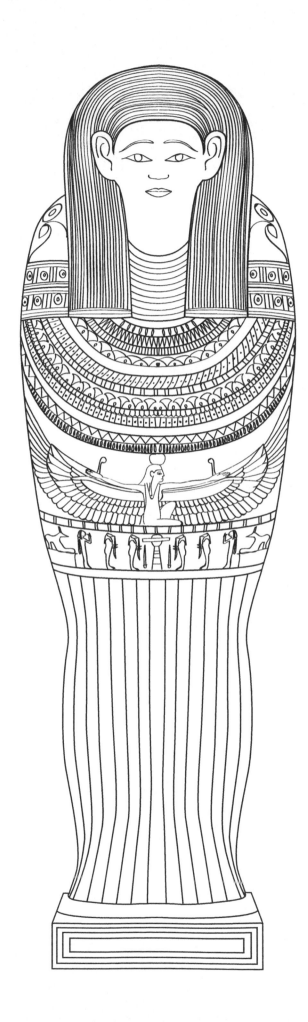

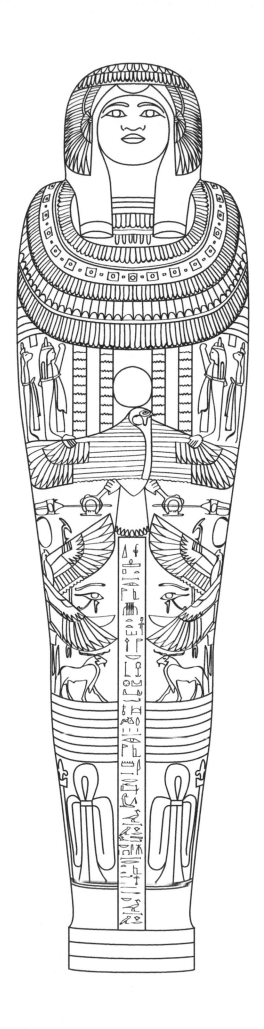

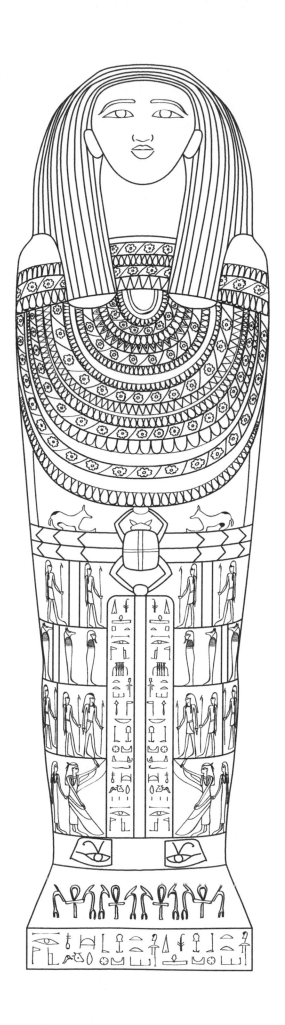

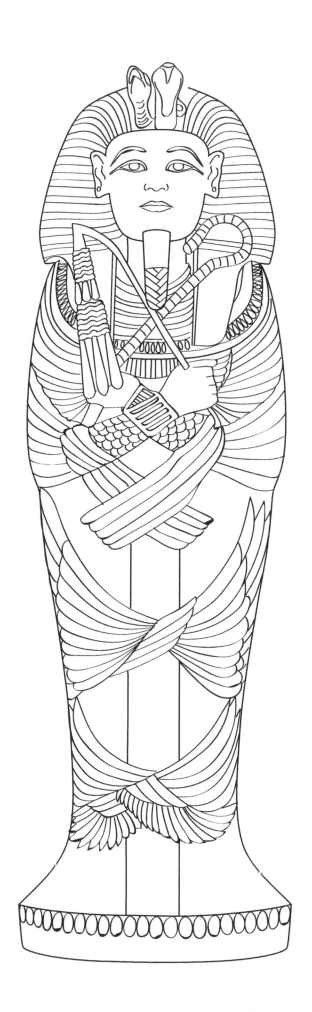

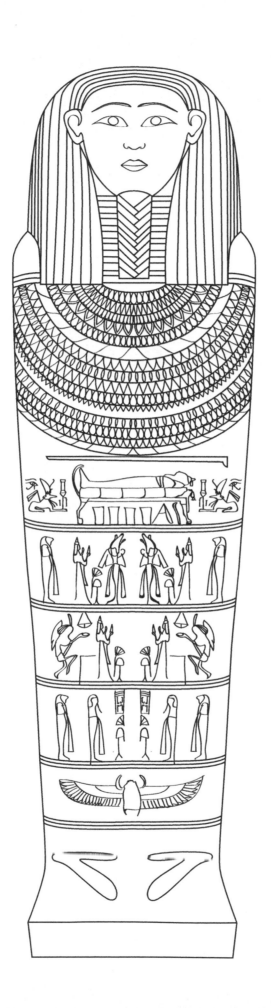

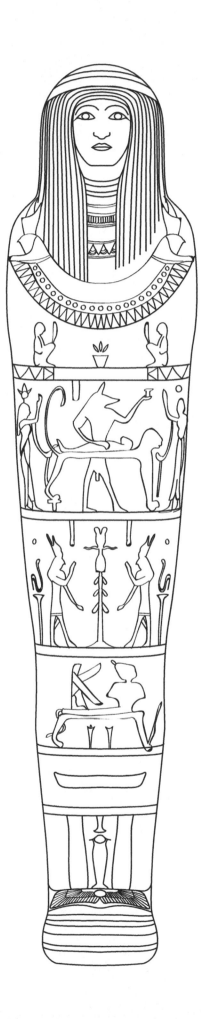

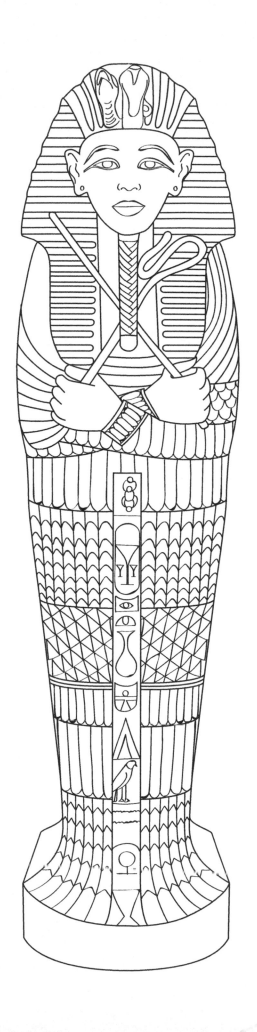

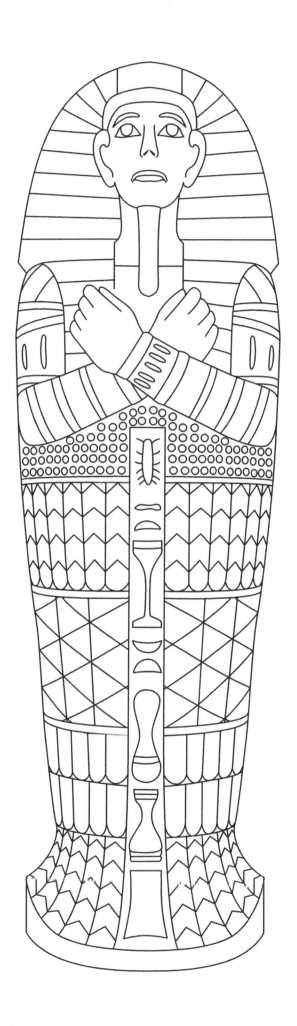

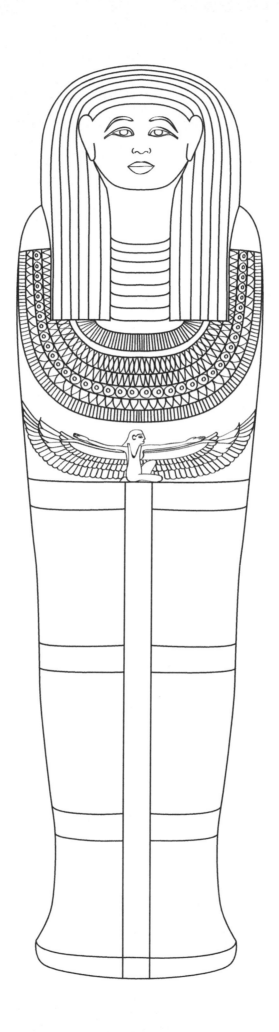

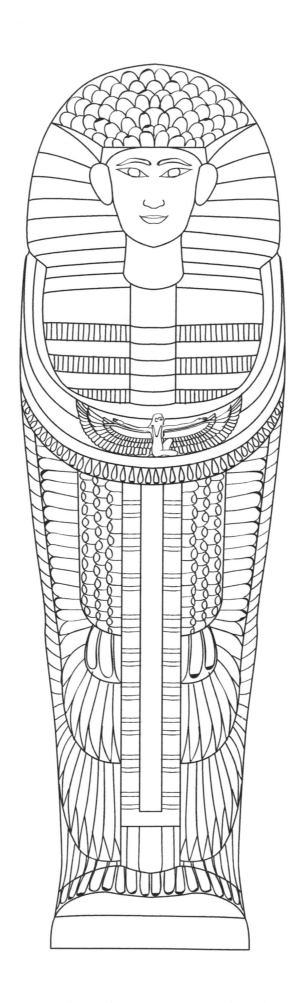

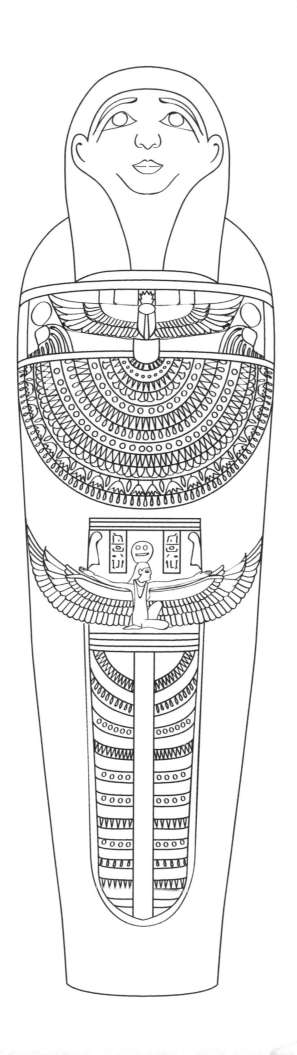

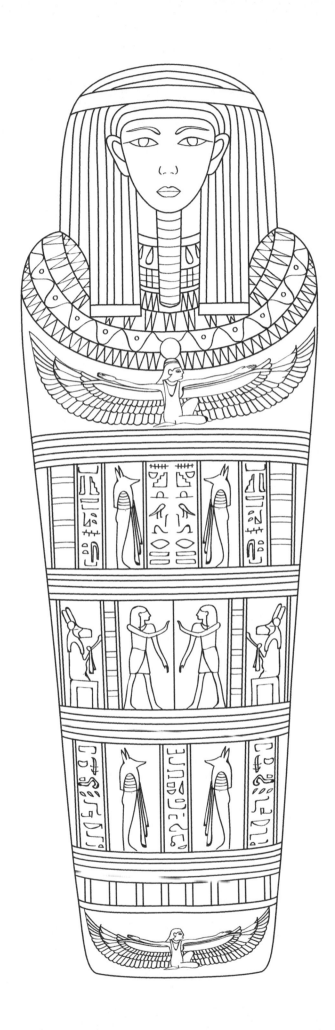

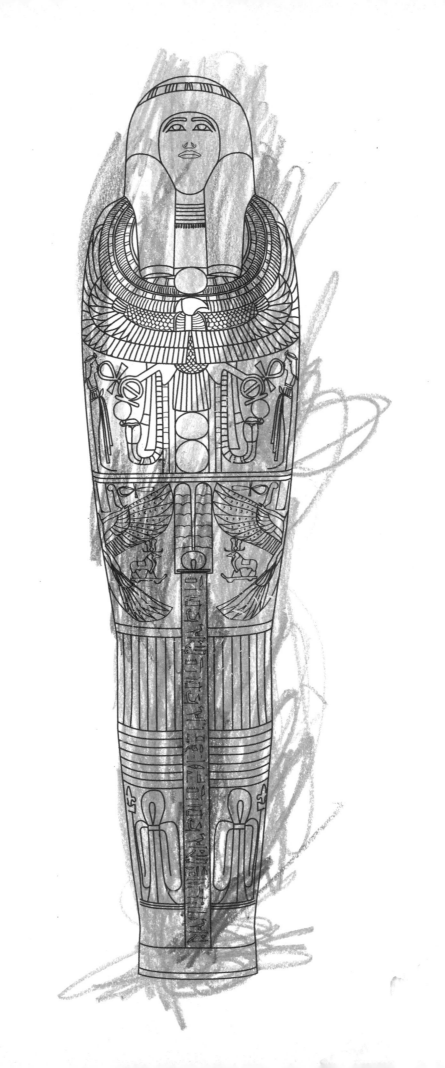

Made in the USA
Las Vegas, NV
16 November 2020